Ripley's———

Believe It or Not!®

TIME
WARP 2

The past and present
collide... again!

Vice President, Licensing & Publishing Amanda Joiner
Editorial Director   Carrie Bolin

Editor   Jessica Firpi
Designer   Mary Eakin
Researcher   James Proud
Proofreader   Rachel Paul
Fact checker   Tracy Green
Reprographics   Bob Prohaska

Published by Ripley Publishing 2019

10 9 8 7 6 5 4 3 2 1

ISBN 978-1-60991-285-7

Library of Congress Control Number: 2019942238

Manufactured in China in May 2019.
First Printing

For more information regarding permission, contact:
VP Licensing & Publishing
Ripley Entertainment Inc.
7576 Kingspointe Parkway
Suite 188
Orlando, Florida 32819
Email: publishing@ripleys.com
www.ripleys.com/books

WARNING
Some of the stunts and activities are undertaken by
experts and should not be attempted by anyone
without adequate training and supervision.

PUBLISHER'S NOTE
While every effort has been made to verify the
accuracy of the entries in this book, the Publisher
cannot be held responsible for any errors contained
in the work. They would be glad to receive any
information from readers.

Ripley's Believe It or Not!

TIME WARP 2

The past and present collide... again!

RIPLEY
PUBLISHING

a Jim Pattison Company

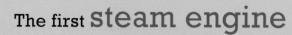

The first steam engine was built more than 60 years before the American Revolution began.

1698

The Milky Way

galaxy existed for approximately

9.1 billion years

before Earth appeared.

The last **public hanging** in the United States took place the same year

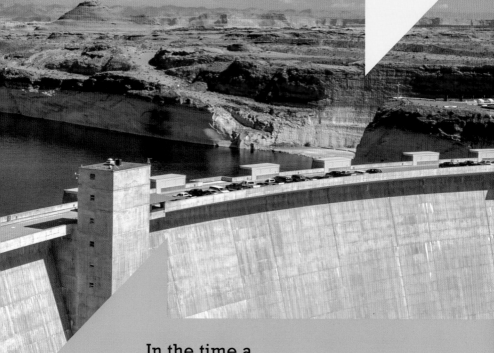

the **Hoover Dam** was completed.

1936

In the time a
50-year-old person
has been alive, the
population of the world
has more than doubled.

The **nautilus** has been on Earth for

290 million years

longer than mammals.

The **universal** **credit card** came before the plastic Hula-Hoop.

1950 vs. 1958

The ATM came before the debit card.

Shawn Mendes was three years old when the **iPod** was released.

2001

The extinct sea creatures
trilobites lived for more than
250 million years—
longer than **dinosaurs**
existed on Earth.

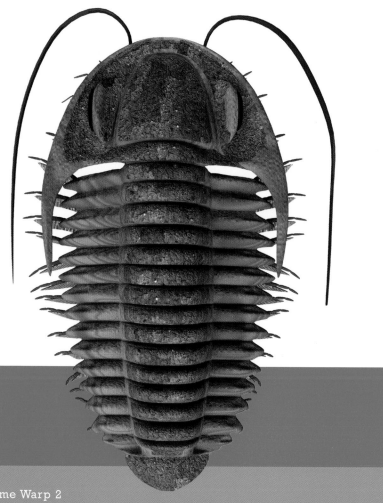

The first *Mario Bros.*
video game was released the same year as
Microsoft Word.
1983

The final episode of *Friends*
aired the same year
Peppa Pig
started.

Power Rangers first appeared the same year Buckingham Palace opened its doors to the public.

1993

1997

PROTECTING
THE EARTH
FROM THE SCUM
OF THE
UNIVERSE

MR. JONES   MR. SMITH
MEN IN BLACK

JULY 2

Men in Black
was released the same year
Princess Diana
died.

The fictional
"Battle of Hogwarts"
happened in May 1998—
the same year Disney's *Mulan*
was released.

The U.S. government is still paying a
Civil War veteran's pension—
more than **150** years
after the war ended.

The Cat in the Hat by Dr. Seuss
was published the year the
Frisbee first went on sale.

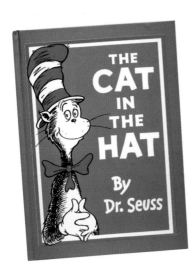

The kingdom of
Ancient Egypt
lasted more than
three times longer
than **England** has existed
as a country.

Batman first appeared six months before the outbreak of World War II.

Ariana Grande
was 13 years old when
Taylor Swift's
first album was released.

2006

Thirty-seven years ago,
E.T. the Extra-Terrestrial
was released.

Thirty-seven years before that,

World War II
ended.

Yo-yos **were played with in** ancient Greece.

500 BC

Fortune cookies
were invented more than 30 years before
Asian immigrants
were legally considered
citizens in the United States.

1914

In February **1930,** **Pluto** was discovered. One month later, **frozen food** went on sale for the first time.

One month after that, Twinkies were invented, and 13 days later the *Looney Tunes* cartoon series made its debut.

WALL ST

The New York Stock Exchange
began the year Beethoven
took his first music lesson.

1792

The Louvre Museum
opened before the
top hat existed.

Contact lenses
were invented before aspirin.

Women in **Liechtenstein** were not allowed to vote in national elections until 1984— more than 60 years after the 19th Amendment was passed in the United States.

Pixar's *The Incredibles* and the *World of Warcraft* video game were both released in 2004.

Root beer was first sold in the United States almost 10 years before peanut butter was invented.

1876
vs.
1884

Hulk Hogan made his professional wrestling debut the year **John Cena** was born.

1977

Teddy bears
are older than Dr. Seuss.

When **Tarzan** first appeared in print, **Harriet Tubman** was still alive.

The Little Mermaid
is older than you think...

1989

It was released 20 years after the moon landing, but it's been more than 30 years since the movie's release.

Steve Jobs and Bill Gates
were born the same year.

1955

A few
Civil War veterans
lived to see the Korean War in

1950–

85 years after

the Civil War ended!

Klondike ice cream bars
were invented in
1922—
the same year a radio was first installed in
the White House.

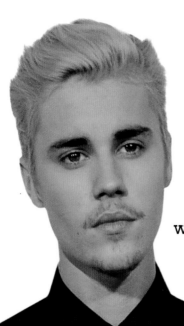

Amazon
was founded the same year
Justin Bieber
was born.

1994

amazon

Disney's *Sleeping Beauty* movie was released the same year Hawaii became the 50th U.S. state.

1959

The
refrigerator
was invented
more than a century
before **canned
beer.**

1834
vs. 1935

BIRRÉ ★ ÖLU ★ OLUT

TRADITIONALLY BREWED

PREMIUM LAGER

1

BEER

★ ★ ★ ★ ★

SINCE
1879

PREMIUM QUALITY

Alc. 4.5% vol.   e 0.33L

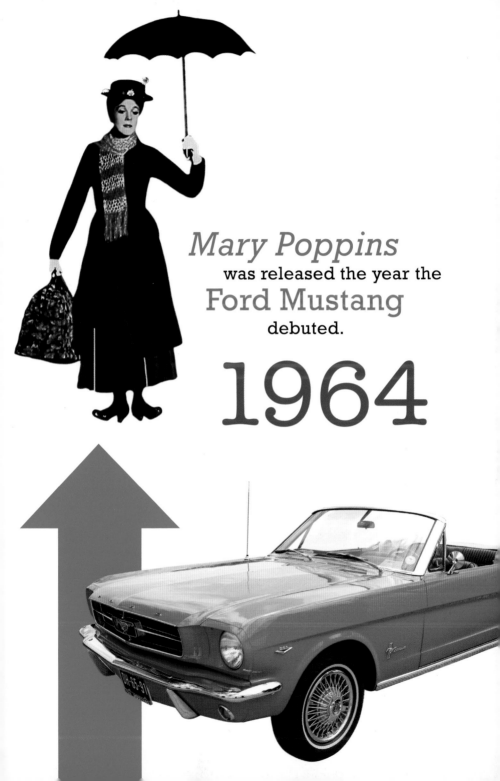

Mary Poppins
was released the year the
Ford Mustang
debuted.

1964

The **teabag**
was invented almost
1,300 years after
tea became popular.

1904
vs. Tang dynasty
(618–907)

1942–2018

Scientists **Steven Hawking** and **Albert Einstein** were both alive at the same time.

1879–1955

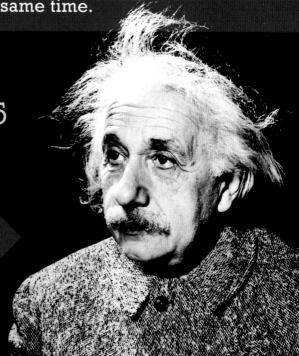

Netflix was founded before Google.

Barcelona soccer club
is older than the country of Australia.

1899 vs. 1901

DC Comics
was founded the year
Donald Duck
made his on-screen debut.

1934

Major League Baseball

had existed for 46 years
when the first season of the
NBA took place.

Bill Murray
is older than **KFC.**

When movie website **IMDb**
first moved to the **World Wide Web,**
it was one of less than 150 other websites.

1993

The coelacanth fish

first appeared about

105–150
million years

before the dinosaurs,
and some species still exist today.

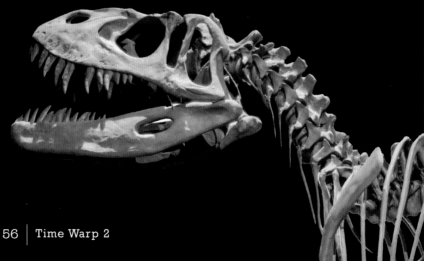

Karate Kid actor **Ralph Macchio** is now older than the actor who played his mentor **Mr. Miyagi**, Pat Morita, when the film was made.

U.S. Olympic gymnast Simone Biles was born the year the first Harry Potter book was published.

1997

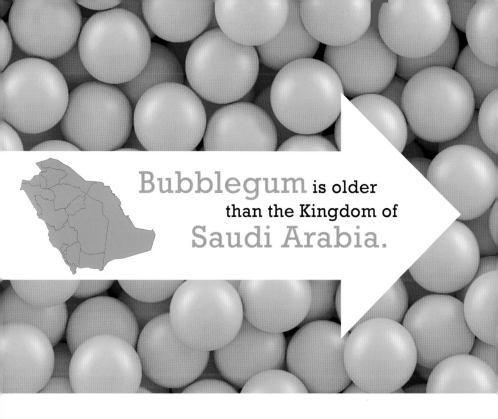

Bubblegum is older than the Kingdom of **Saudi Arabia.**

When the **U.S. Marine Corp** was founded, **warships** still had sails.

The Berlin Wall

has now been down for longer than it was standing.

Zayn Malik was born
the year that *Jurassic Park*
was released in movie theaters.

1993

Beer predates bread.

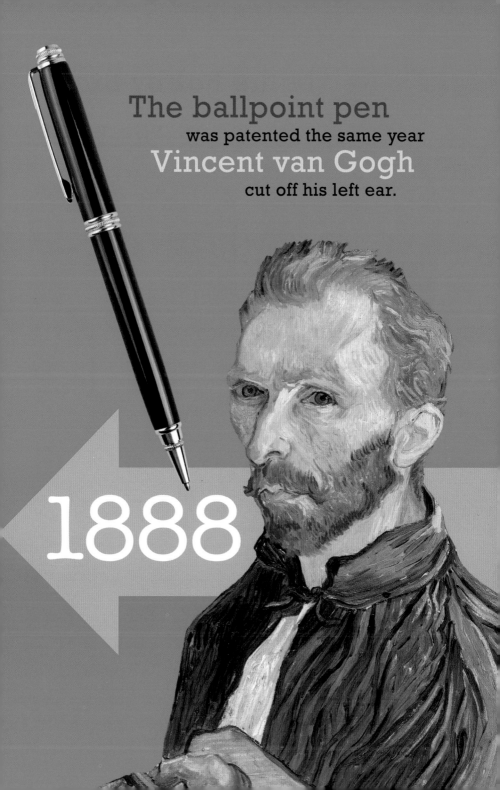

Stranger Things star
Millie Bobby Brown
is the same age as
Facebook.

When the **battery**
was invented,
there were only
16 U.S. states.

Ariana Grande
is the same age as
Beanie Babies.
1993

John Wilkins was the first known person to propose the idea of **space travel** and experimented with making flying machines in the

1650s,

back when reflecting **telescopes** didn't even exist.

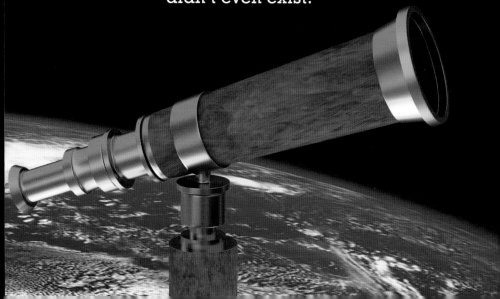

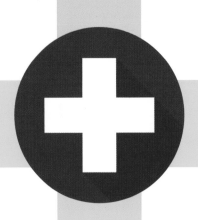

The first army **horse-driven ambulance** debuted the same year as the **guillotine.**

1792

We had **carbonated water**
before we had flushing toilets.

1767 vs.
1775

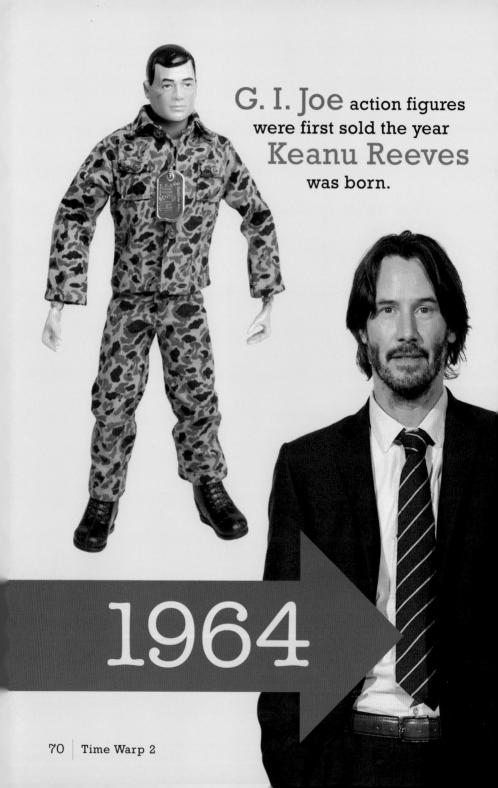

G. I. Joe action figures were first sold the year **Keanu Reeves** was born.

1964

Spain
ruled parts of North America
for longer than the
United States
has been an independent country.

1492-1898 (406 years)
vs.
1776 (243 years)

Nicolas Cage
and *Jeopardy!*
are the same age.

1964

$50,000

When the country of
Iceland was first settled,
there were still wild lions in Europe.

Legendary scientist **Albert Einstein** died the same year that the first **McDonald's** opened.

1955

Will Smith is now older than the actor who played his uncle in *The Fresh Prince of Bel-Air*, James Avery, when the series started in 1990.

Amelia Earhart went missing the same year as the first televised **baseball game.**

Watching *Aladdin* today is like watching

The Sound of Music when *Aladdin* was first released.

2019 – 1992 – 1965

(27 years between each film)

NASA was formed the same year as IHOP.

1958

When **Columbus** landed in America, the population of **Spain** was less than that of modern-day New York.

The Wizard of Oz

movie was released a few days before **WWII** began in 1939.

Slot machines were invented before **Las Vegas** existed.

During the time of the
dinosaurs,
a day was approximately
23 hours, not 24.

In 1964, the game *Operation* was invented and **Martin Luther King Jr.** won the Nobel Peace Prize.

The band
Green Day
formed a year after
Lady Gaga
was born.

1987

Jay-Z's
first album
and the first
Game of Thrones
book were released
in the same year.

1996

The **computer mouse** was invented the same year as Buffalo wings.

1964

We put men on the **moon** before we put wheels on **luggage.**

Television is older than FM radio.

1926 vs. 1933

The **first telephone book** was issued on February 21, **1878,** in New Haven, Connecticut, and featured only 50 names.

1781

Los Angeles was founded the year the planet **Uranus** was discovered.

The Nightmare before Christmas
was released closer in time...

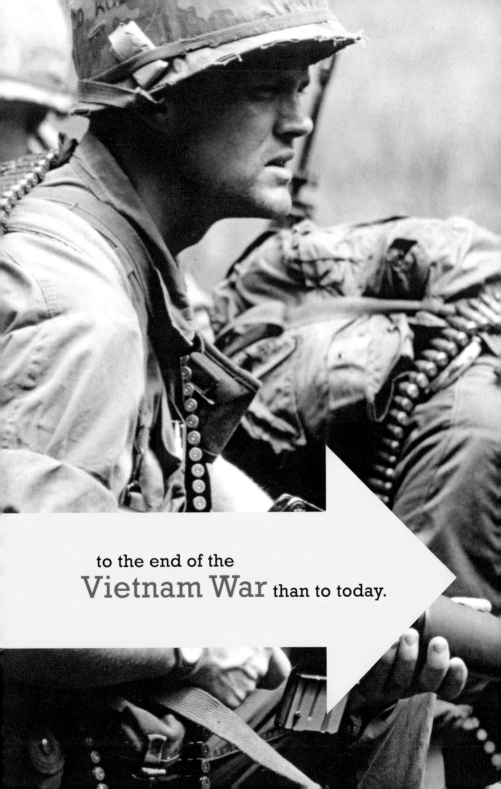

to the end of the
Vietnam War than to today.

The Chinchorro people

of South America were
mummifying their dead

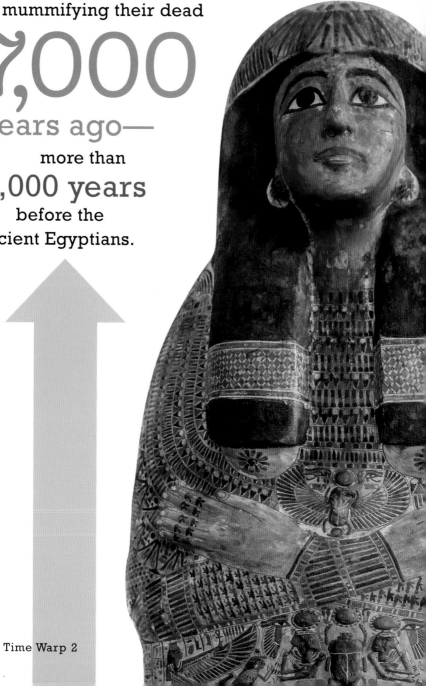

7,000

years ago—

more than

2,000 years

before the
ancient Egyptians.

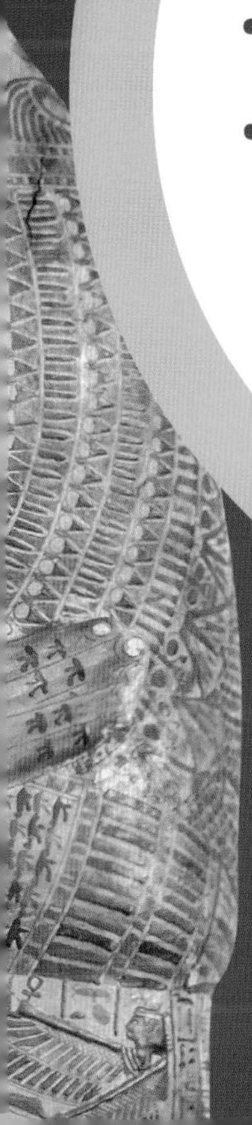

When the
printing press
was invented

in 1440,

the Holy Roman
Empire still existed.

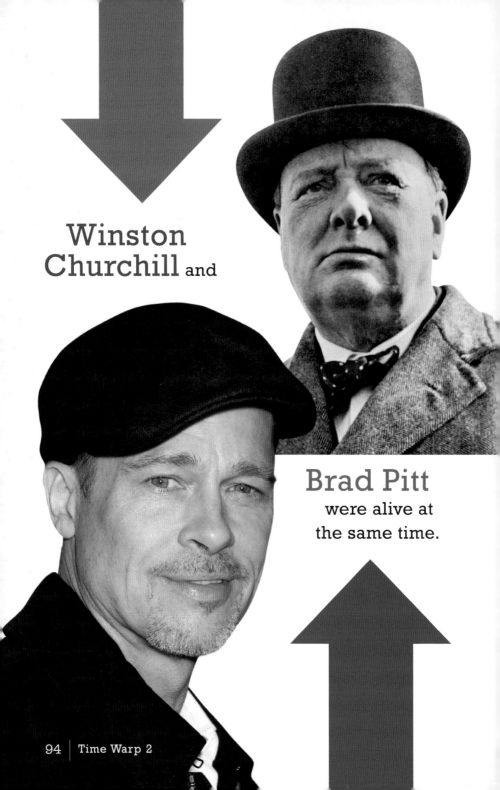

Winston
Churchill and

Brad Pitt
were alive at
the same time.

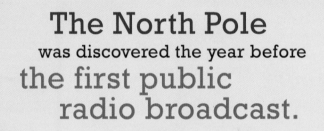

The North Pole
was discovered the year before
the first public
radio broadcast.

Star Wars actor Harrison Ford is older than cable television.

The telephone
was invented the year
bananas became popular
in the United States.

1876

- -

There are more Indian people
alive today
than there were humans
on the planet in
1800.

Microchips were invented the same year **LEGO bricks** were patented.

1958

The first car was built in France before the American Revolutionary War... but it would be

125 years

before someone added a steering wheel to automobiles.

The London Underground subway

opened the same year that...

Abraham Lincoln
issued the Emancipation Proclamation in
1863.

There have been
12 United States presidents
since *The Tonight Show*
first aired.

Daniel Radcliffe
is the same age as the
World Wide Web.
1989

Dinosaurs
were on Earth for about
500 times longer
than humans have existed.

When **Peter Pan** made
his first appearance in print,
the **Wright brothers**
hadn't flown a plane yet.

1901 vs. 1902

In **1839,**
the **first selfie**
was taken, and the
slang word "O.K."
was invented in the
Boston Morning Post
newspaper.

Kanye West
released his debut album
the month that
Facebook
went live for the first time.

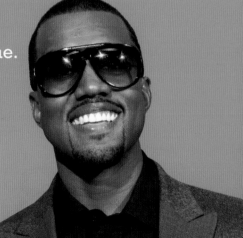

POSTS

happyuser
5 mins ·

I am #happy

2004

Tap to tag a location

Like   Comment   Share

Write a comment...

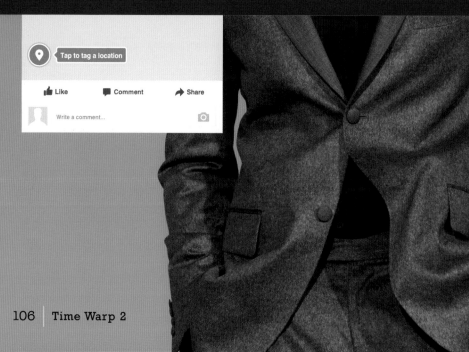

BOSTON

1897

The first
Boston Marathon
took place the year
Dracula was published.

RAINBOW ROOM

O·B·S·E·R·V·A·T·I·O·N

D·E·C·K

NBC STUDIOS

1975

Comedy sketch show *SNL* debuted the same year as *Jaws*.

Dr. Pepper
is older than
Coca-Cola.

Car **windshield wipers**
were invented just five years after
electric headlights
were introduced. **1903**

When the first
World Series
took place,
Russia still had a tsar.
1903

People were playing **hopscotch** when **America** was still a **British colony.**

1903

Harley-Davidson motorcycles were founded the same year as the first **Tour de France.**

Cell phone maker Nokia was originally founded the year before the Civil War ended.

The first successful mechanical calculator was built almost 320 years before the electronic version.

1642

A Christmas Story was released the same year as *Star Wars: Return of the Jedi.*

1983

Meghan Markle was born the same month MTV was launched.

August
1981

French's
yellow mustard
first appeared the same year
that Gillette razor
blades were patented.

1904

The first 3D movie was released the same year King Tut's tomb was discovered.

1922

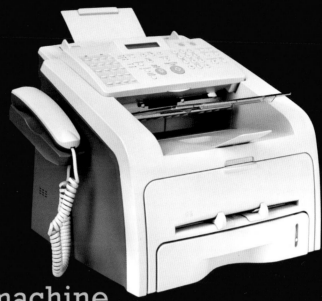

The fax machine was invented before the telephone.

On New York City's 250th anniversary, Las Vegas did not exist.

The Dixon Ticonderoga pencil company, based in Florida, was founded 50 years before the state became part of the United States.

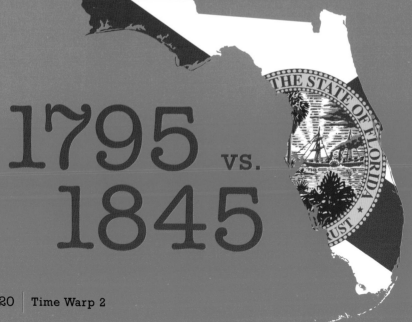

1795 vs. 1845

Lucky Charms
are the same age as
Sandra Bullock.

1964

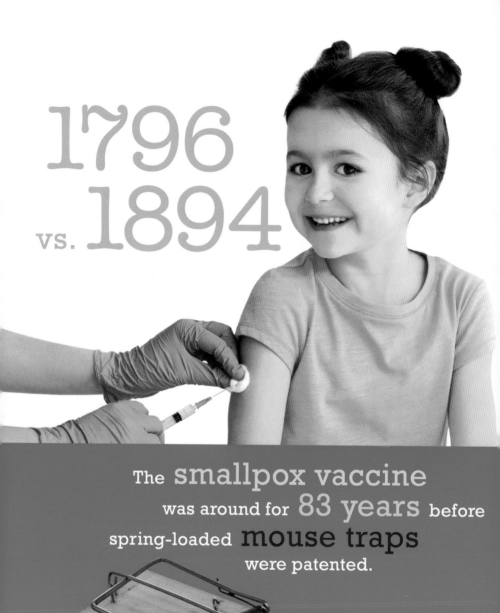

1796 vs. 1894

The **smallpox vaccine** was around for 83 years before spring-loaded **mouse traps** were patented.

The first pizzeria
in America opened 55 years
before Domino's.

1905 vs.
1960

The **saxophone** was invented the same year the **Smithsonian** was established.

1846

The Hollywood sign was erected the same year the Walt Disney Company was founded.

The Internet and *Sesame Street* are the same age.

1969

The first odometer
(mileage counter) was invented nearly

2,000 years before
the gas-powered car.

Oranges were named **hundreds of years** before the word came to mean the color orange.

Leonardo Di Caprio

is the same age as Skittles.

1974

When **Hillary Clinton** was born,
Israel did not exist.

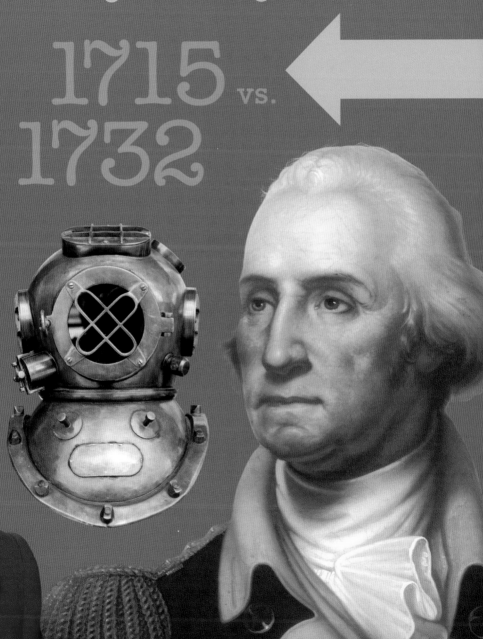

The first **diving suits** were invented before **George Washington** was born.

1715 vs. 1732

The gunfight at the O.K. Corral in Tombstone, Arizona, on October 26, 1881— the **most famous shootout** in the American Old West—lasted only 30 seconds.

Romania did not have **color television** until 1985, the year *The Care Bears* TV series began.

Land plants existed for approximately
220–370 million years...

before they developed flowers.

PEZ candy

debuted the same year construction started on

Mount Rushmore.

1927

1870 vs. 1871

Charles Dickens died in 1870, and one year later, the first **pinball machine** was patented.

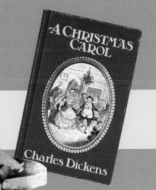

When air conditioning
was invented, there was no such thing as
fingerprinting
for criminal investigations.

331 years separate
the founding of Floridian cities
St. Augustine and Miami.

1565 vs.
1896

There were blue jeans
before there were earmuffs.

Spalding Sporting Goods
and the telephone
are the same age.

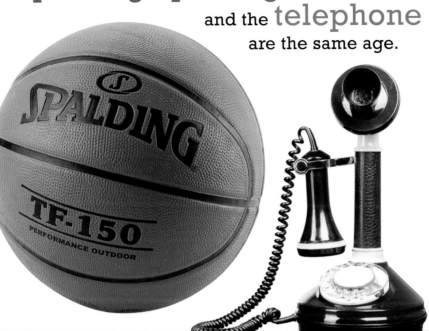

1876

Email existed for 20 years
before the World Wide Web.

1971 vs. 1991

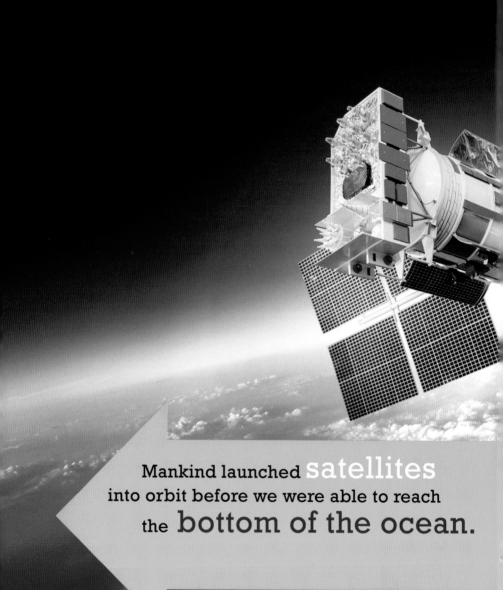

Mankind launched satellites into orbit before we were able to reach the bottom of the ocean.

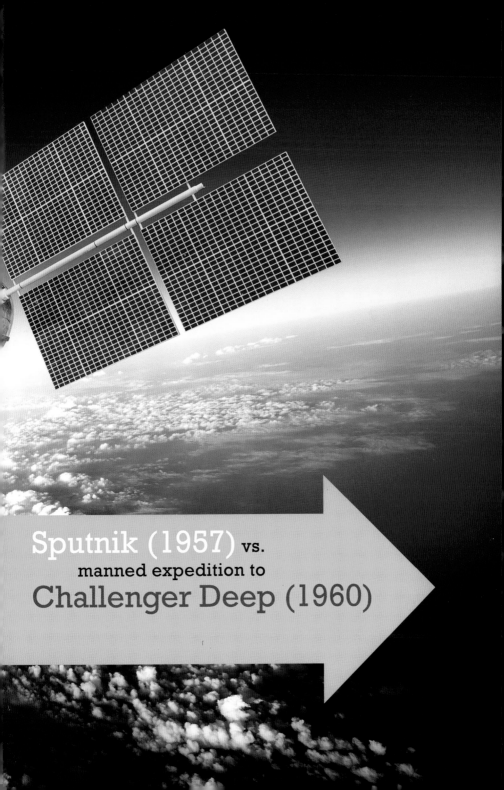

Sputnik (1957) vs. manned expedition to Challenger Deep (1960)

In 1997,

Grand Theft Auto was first released, and the Teletubbies made their first television appearance.

Paper planes existed before planes.

The Montreal Canadiens hockey team is older than the NHL itself.

Acknowledgments

8 Steve Bloom Images/Alamy Stock Photo; 14 (tr) Tal Revivo/Alamy Stock Vector, (b) PictureLux/The Hollywood Archive/Alamy Stock Photo; 16 (r) Moviestore collection Ltd/Alamy Stock Photo; 17 (tl) Photo 12/Alamy Stock Photo, (br) age fotostock/Alamy Stock Photo; 19 (b) Allstar Picture Library/Alamy Stock Photo; 20 (bl) flab/Alamy Stock Photo; 26–27 (dp) The Advertising Archives/Alamy Stock Photo; 39 (tl) Historic Collection/Alamy Stock Photo, (br) Glasshouse Images/Alamy Stock Photo; 40–41 (dp) Moviestore collection Ltd/Alamy Stock Photo; 47 (l) AF archive/Alamy Stock Photo; 49 (tl) Allstar Picture Library/Alamy Stock Photo; 51 (tl) dpa picture alliance/Alamy Live News, (br) MARKA/Alamy Stock Photo; 53 (br) MARKA/Alamy Stock Photo; 54 (tl) 360b/Alamy Stock Photo, (br) © Miguel Candela/SOPA Images via ZUMA Wire; 57 (cl) United Archives GmbH/Alamy Stock Photo; 58 (l) sjbooks/Alamy Stock Photo; 60 AF archive/Alamy Stock Photo; 61 (l) The Advertising Archives/Alamy Stock Photo; 65 (bc) Art Directors & TRIP/Alamy Stock Photo; 70 (l) Chris Willson/Alamy Stock Photo; 74 (br) B Christopher/Alamy Stock Photo; 75 NBC/Album/Alamy Stock Photo; 77 (t) MARKA/Alamy Stock Photo, (b) Photo 12/Alamy Stock Photo; 80 (b) World History Archive/Alamy Stock Photo; 83 (l) CBW/Alamy Stock Photo; 84 (tr) CBW/Alamy Stock Photo; 86 (t) Public Domain {{PD-US}} NASA; 90 United Archives GmbH/Alamy Stock Photo; 94 (tr) Ian Dagnall/Alamy Stock Photo; 95 (tc) Created by Mary Eakin; 104 (b) Lebrecht Music & Arts/Alamy Stock Photo; 110 (l) World History Archive/Alamy Stock Photo; 112 (t) Oleksiy Maksymenko Photography/Alamy Stock Photo; 114 (b) AF archive/Alamy Stock Photo; 125 Moviestore collection Ltd/Alamy Stock Photo; 127 (sp) WENN Rights Ltd/Alamy Stock Photo; 131 (sp) United Archives GmbH/Alamy Stock Photo; 135 (tr) Panther Media GmbH/Alamy Stock Photo, (bl) GL Archive/Alamy Stock Photo, (br) DWD-Media/Alamy Stock Photo

Key: t = top, b = bottom, c = center, l = left, r = right, sp = single page, dp = double page, bkg = background

All other photos are from Shutterstock.com.

Every attempt has been made to acknowledge correctly and contact copyright holders, and we apologize in advance for any unintentional errors or omissions, which will be corrected in future editions.

Stop by our website daily for new stories, photos, contests, and more!
www.ripleys.com

 /RipleysBelieveItOrNot

 @Ripleys

 youtube.com/Ripleys

 @RipleysBelieveItOrNot